THE NATIONAL AUDUBON SOCIETY COLLECTION
NATURE SERIES

NORTH AMERICAN
WILDFLOWERS

THE NATIONAL AUDUBON SOCIETY COLLECTION
NATURE SERIES™

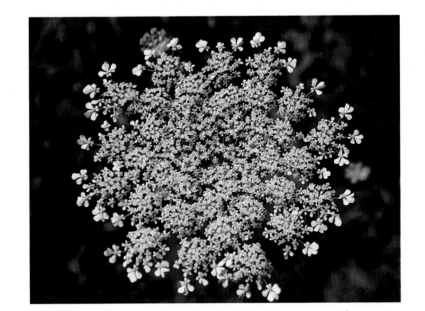

NORTH AMERICAN
WILDFLOWERS

Text by Barbara Burn

*Foreword by David K. Northington, Executive Director,
National Wildflower Research Center*

Bonanza Books · New York

All of the photographs in this book are from Photo Researchers/National Audubon Society Collection. The name of the individual photographer follows each caption.

Photographers' credits for uncaptioned photographs in the front and back matter of this book are (in order of appearance): Russ Kinne, Russ Kinne, Townsend P. Dickinson, Pat & Tom Leeson, Richard H. Smith, Mary M. Thacher, Peter Fink, Constance Porter, Noble Proctor, Bob & Elsie Boggs, Earl Roberge, George E. Jones III, Tom Branch, Tom McHugh, Russ Kinne, Joe DiStefano, Richard Jepperson, S. J. Krasemann, Frank J. Miller, Dr. Robert H. Potts Jr, Maude Dorr, and Robert C. Hermes.

The National Audubon Society Collection Nature Series
Staff for this book
General Editor: Robin Corey
Photo Researcher: Nancy Golden
Production Editor: Philip Madans
Designer: June Marie Bennett
Production Manager: Laura Torrecilla
Production Supervisor: Cindy Lake

This 1984 edition is published by Bonanza Books, distributed by Crown Publishers, Inc., 225 Park Avenue South, New York, New York 10003
THE NATIONAL AUDUBON SOCIETY COLLECTION NATURE SERIES is a trademark owned by the National Audubon Society, Inc.

Manufactured in Italy

Library of Congress Cataloging in Publication Data

Burn, Barbara.
North American wildflowers
(The National Audubon Society collection nature series)
Includes index.
1. Wildflowers—North America.
I. Title.   II. Title: North American wildflowers.   III. Series.
QK110.B87   1984   582.13′097   84-12280

ISBN: 0-517-447401

h g f e d c b

THE NATIONAL AUDUBON SOCIETY AND ITS MISSION

In the late 1800s, forward-thinking people became concerned over the slaughter of plumed birds for the millinery trade. They gathered together in groups to protest, calling themselves Audubon societies after the famous painter and naturalist John James Audubon. In 1905, thirty-five state Audubon groups incorporated as the National Association of Audubon Societies for the Protection of Wild Birds and Animals, since shortened to National Audubon Society. Now, with more than half a million members, five hundred chapters, ten regional offices, a twenty-five million dollar budget, and a staff of two hundred seventy-three, the Audubon Society is a powerful force for conservation research, education, and action.

The Society's headquarters are in New York City: the legislative branch works out of an office on Capitol Hill in Washington, D.C. Ecology camps, environmental education centers, research stations, and eighty sanctuaries are strategically located around the country. The Society publishes a prize-winning magazine. *Audubon:* an ornithological journal, *American Birds:* a newspaper of environmental issues and Society activities, *Audubon Action:* and a newsletter as part of the youth education program, *Audubon Adventures.*

The Society's mission is expressed by the Audubon Cause: to conserve plants and animals and their habitats, to further the wise use of land and water, to promote rational energy strategies, to protect life from pollution, and to seek solutions to global environmental problems.

National Audubon Society 950 Third Avenue New York, New York 10022

CONTENTS

FOREWORD

Sometimes, when I am happily alone in a beautiful natural setting replete with the color and diversity of some of the many species of North American wildflowers, I have the sensation that only I alone have been fortunate enough to witness this example of nature's creativity. In a sense, this is true; in an hour, even a few minutes, there will be subtle changes; flowers will open or close and, thus, my moment *will* have been unique in time.

Although the beauty and solitude of these moments are wonderfully relaxing, it is at these moments that I also want to share what I see and what I feel. The rush of sensations resulting from this display are totally encompassing and have the capability of washing away the seemingly trivial concerns and responsibilities of day-to-day existence.

I realize that I am not the only person who has felt those sensations any more than I am the only person who has seen an attractive vista of wildflowers. Few of our natural wonders strike a more responsive chord than wildflowers. They are esthetically pleasing in their appearance and biologically amazing in their continued hardy existence. Their potential for beautification, landscaping, and land reclamation is significant, both for their beauty as well as for the potential for economic savings in such areas as watering and maintenance.

Equally important, however, is their stubborn presence. Through drought, flood, freezing, or blisteringly hot conditions, they appear in their appropriate season. For this I am always grateful to nature's adaptive diversity. The more I learn about the distributions, ecological requirements, reproductive strategies, and resilience of flowering plants, the more I appreciate their delicate beauty and unending variety of color and design.

When browsing through bookstores I am always slightly disappointed that, particularly in comparison to the thousands of books available on other topics, there are relatively few books on wildflowers. Fortunately, there are increasing numbers of such works and I eagerly examine each new one that appears. Some are photographs only, others are field guides with technical information. The balanced combination of selected wildflower photographs from the National Audubon Society Collection and the informative, readable text by Barbara Burn results in a book appealing to the eye and to the mind. The beauty of our North American wildflowers is only enhanced by a basic knowledge of their structure, function, ecology, and utility. Regardless of the region of the country in which you live, this book will provide an enticing sample of the wildflowers available to you.

Aldo Leopold began the foreword to his classic, *A Sand County Alamanac,* by stating, "There are some who can live without wild things, and some who cannot." I encourage the readers of this book to be among the latter, to actively appreciate the beauty of our wildflower natural heritage, to help preserve and enjoy this resource, and to find *your* unique moments of peace and beauty.

DAVID K. NORTHINGTON
Executive Director
National Wildflower Research Center

Austin, Texas
1984

NORTH AMERICAN
WILDFLOWERS

INTRODUCTION

One of nature's loveliest sights is a field in springtime filled with colorful flowers, creating patterns of blue, lavender, yellow, pink, and white as far as the eye can see. These delicate blossoms, which may last from only a day to a few weeks at most, seem to be incredibly fragile at first glance, with no sturdy trunks to support them and few defense mechanisms to protect them from harm. Yet wildflowers are very hardy, indeed. They must be, since the function they perform is essential to the very continuation of plant life. Although gardeners think of flowers as decorative assets in the backyard or home, botanists know that they are perhaps the most crucial element in every flowering plant. The roots of a plant secure it in the earth and absorb nutrients and water to sustain it, while the leaves take in the sunlight and manufacture the energy that enables the plant to grow, but the flower is the reproductive organ, producing the seeds that will ensure the future of the species. Though we admire a flower's particular color, shape, or odor for its own sake, we may not realize that each of these elements plays a significant role in enabling the plant to reproduce its own kind.

The immense variation in wildflowers may serve the purpose of delighting the eye of the casual beholder, but in fact nature's purpose is much more basic—that of survival—and each variation is simply an individual plant's way of responding to the special conditions under which it grows. There are more than fifty thousand species of flowering plants in the world (this group includes trees and grasses as well as what we commonly think of as wildflowers) and they have adapted to nearly every sort of habitat on earth, from the arid desert and windblown mountaintop to the lush rain forest or rich meadowland. In this book, we will visit some of these regions on the North American continent and take a closer look at some of the flowers that grow there to see

how the different conditions of soil, rainfall, and temperature have affected the appearance of these beautiful living things. After seeing how some plants can cope with virtually no water, sun, or even soil, it will be difficult to think of wildflowers as the frail and helpless plants that they appear to be.

THE FLOWER

Although each flowering species seems to be very different from the next, the function of each flower is exactly the same—to produce fertile seed. Like animals, each plant has a set of reproductive organs, male and female. Most flowers contain both sexual organs, the stamen (male) and pistil (female), which are supported, protected, or displayed by petals. These petals are in turn supported by a calyx, which is a group of specialized leaves called sepals. The stamen has two distinct sections: the filament, or stalk, that holds up the anther, the organ that produces and stores pollen. The pistil has three main parts: the ovary at the base, which produces ovules, or unfertilized seeds; the stigma, which receives the pollen; and the style, which connects the ovary to the stigma and serves as a pathway for the pollen as it travels to the ovary. Once the pollen fertilizes the ovules, the ovary develops into a seed container, which can take one of many different forms, such as a pod, nut, berry, grain, or fleshy fruit. These seed containers—also called fruits—are then dispersed by one means or another so that

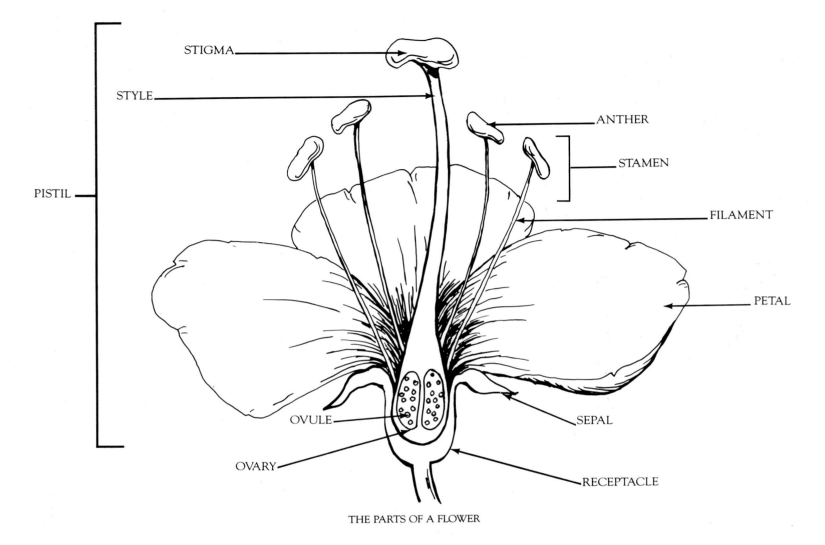

STIGMA

STYLE

PISTIL

ANTHER

STAMEN

FILAMENT

PETAL

OVULE

SEPAL

OVARY

RECEPTACLE

THE PARTS OF A FLOWER

new plants may begin growing elsewhere. For some plants, animals do the dispersing (squirrels burying nuts, birds eating grain or berries and spreading the seeds to distant locations), while some merely drop their fruits to the ground nearby and the wind carries the seeds to a suitable spot where growing conditions will enable the seeds to germinate and form new plants.

Many flowers contain both male and female organs, but since self-pollination would result in weak new plants because of inbreeding, nature has arranged in most cases for the stamen and pistil to mature at different times. This means, of course, that two or more plants are needed to produce fertile seeds. The methods of pollination are varied, and this fact is what makes the appearance of flowers

differ so greatly from one species to another. Flowers that must depend on insects or birds to carry pollen from the anther of one plant to the stamen of another are usually colored in such a way that they will attract the animals who will do the job. Honeybees, for instance, are attracted to colors that they can see—yellow, orange, blue, and lavender—while hummingbirds and butterflies seem to be drawn to reddish flowers. Moths, on the other hand, prefer white or light-colored flowers that bloom at night and have a distinct fragrance, while flies seem to be attracted to plants that produce a decaying aroma, such as skunk cabbage. These animals do not, of course, provide the pollination service intentionally; they visit flowers in search of food, usually the nectar that the flower produces, and they

accidentally pick up pollen on their bodies and transport it to a waiting stigma on the next flower they visit.

Not all plants rely on animals for pollination but use the wind to carry pollen (which can cause great distress to humans suffering from hay fever); these plants rarely have elaborate, colored petals or distinctive aromas since they needn't attract anyone. Grasses native to the windswept plains are pollinated by wind, and though they produce flowers they are rarely thought of as flowering plants by the average observer since their blossoms are not at all showy. Cattails and pussy willows, too, depend on wind to carry pollen, producing furry stigmas to catch it in the air.

Although the basic elements of each flower are essentially the same, there are enormous variations in shape as well as in color and odor (or the lack of it). Some flowers are solitary, each one growing on an individual stem, such as the trillium, while other flowers grow in clusters on a single stem. As you look at the photographs in this book, observe the many different forms these multiple flowers take. Some grow directly on the stem itself, while others grow on branches; some grow so closely together that they appear to be a single flower. The daisy and clover, for instance, are not solitary flowers at all but heads containing a large number of tiny blossoms. Leaves, too, vary considerably. Some leaves are smooth-edged with parallel veins, while others have complex shapes and a network of veins. In the jack-in-the-pulpit, for instance, what appears to be a petal is actually a leaf that surrounds the small flowers within.

Another important difference between flowers involves lifespan. Some flowers are annuals, growing from seed to plant to flower to seed in a single season, after which the plant itself dies. The seed remains dormant for the winter—or longer if growing conditions are not suitable— and then germinates, producing a new plant the following year. Biennial plants live for two years, growing the stalk and leaves the first year and flowering the second year. Perennial plants can live for many years; some retain their aboveground growth, including stem and leaves, during the winter, but many perennials drop them and remain dormant underground in one of various forms. A bulb, such as that seen in crocuses, is an underground bud that will send out new shoots in spring; a corm is a type of underground stem, while a rhizome is a horizontal, rootlike stem that sends out roots below and shoots above. These growths are used to store nutrients to keep the plant alive when it is not absorbing or manufacturing its own food, and many animals and humans have found them to be valuable sources of nourishment.

Scientists who have studied these myriad differences between plants over the years have classified them according to type, grouping similar plants in specific families. Yet, to the average observer, closely related plants can appear to be quite different. The composite family, the largest family of all, containing nearly half of all flowering plants, is represented by such different species as the thistle, dandelion, and daisy. And some plants that look alike, such as the wood sorrel and the spring beauty, are actually very different and unrelated, scientifically speaking. Part of the reason for these apparent similarities may be that the flowers exist in the same woodland habitat and must make certain adaptations to deal with similar situations—availability of light, rainfall, and so on. Some wildflowers are so adaptable that they can grow almost anywhere, and because they are so hardy, they may even interfere with other plants. When they interfere with gardens or agriculture, we tend to call them weeds and spend a great deal of money and effort getting rid of them. Some weeds, however, are lovely and in certain settings are quite desirable. We will read about and see these plants in the last chapter; growing along roadsides and in vacant lots, their colorful blossoms help to beautify otherwise unattractive locations.

WILDFLOWERS AT WORK

As far as naturalists are concerned, the great value of wildflowers is in perpetuating the species, in contributing their very presence to the environment in which they play an integral part, though their particular function may not be well understood, even by botanists. Where certain habitats have been disturbed by the construction of dams or human habitations or by the cultivation of land for farms and forestry, some flowers have declined in numbers, occasionally becoming endangered species or even extinct altogether. The trailing arbutus, for example, is especially sensitive to such disturbances and has become very scarce in the woodlands of the eastern half of the North American continent. It is important, therefore, for amateur naturalists to leave

such plants where they are, rather than to pick them or attempt to transplant them to their own gardens. Some wildflowers make lovely garden plants and are easy to grow—daisies, violets, asters, and buttercups are especially popular and are not at all endangered in the wild—and a pretty wildflower garden can turn any backyard into a showplace. But it is always best to purchase the seeds from a commercial nursery or seed catalog company rather than try to collect flowers from nature. It is not always easy to reproduce growing conditions in which the plant will feel at home, and it would be a shame to risk the loss of a wildflower in this experimental way.

A popular pastime for flower lovers in the days before wildflowers were considered a natural treasure was to collect and press them. Some enthusiasts would fill entire albums or create handsome dried collages or arrangements, and

even today such objects are admired for their beauty. But again, because of the rarity of some flowers and the simple fact that living flowers are always more beautiful than dead ones, collecting them is not recommended. The best ways to bring wildflowers home are through your own photographs or by sketching or painting them on the spot and then displaying your artwork.

Another traditional use of wildflowers has been in the preparation of certain foods and medications, for it is true that many plants have special properties that are considered valuable to humans. Natural-food cookbooks abound with recipes for dandelion wine, crystallized violet candies, thistle salad, and chicory coffee, and beauty books often recommend flowers for their aromatic or astringent qualities. Several plants have become famous for their medicinal benefits, some of them having been discovered by American Indians who found that certain roots, leaves, and flowers served as effective healing agents, laxatives, or remedies for such problems as snakebite. Every human culture has had its herbalists, and every herbalist has had his or her theories; perhaps the most curious theory is the one called the doctrine of signatures, an ancient set of beliefs that recommended plants as treatments for the ailments they resembled. For example, because the purple trillium has an especially foul odor, it was once used to treat gangrene, a foul-smelling disease.

As useful as some plants may be, there are a large number of plants that are considered harmful to man. The well-named death camas of the lily family, which grows in the grasslands of the midwest, is poisonous to livestock and can cause comas in humans. Locoweed, a relative of the delicious clovers and other members of the pea family, is famous for its toxic effect on grazing cattle. Perhaps most interesting in this regard is the nightshade family, which includes not only the poisonous jimsonweed and the deadly nightshade but also plants that produce tomatoes, potatoes, eggplant, bell peppers, and tobacco.

Because humans have found some plants so useful, they have learned to cultivate many species—for food, to feed livestock, to produce garden flowers—and when the early settlers arrived in North America, they often brought plants with them for these purposes. Unfortunately, some of these plants "escaped" and adapted to a life in the wild, often displacing a number of native plants. The water hya-

cinth, for example, once imported from tropical America, is now considered one of our worst weeds, since it has spread rapidly in the southern United States, clogging waterways there. The common dandelion, buttercup, and ox-eye daisy are other imports that have earned the name weed for their ability to grow nearly anywhere, especially where they are not wanted.

OBSERVING WILDFLOWERS

In spite of all of these various uses (and abuses) of wildflower plants, the greatest value they serve us nowadays is in what they can teach us about the intricate and fascinating ways in which the environment works. Although they may not have any obvious part to play in the habitat in which they grow, wildflowers do have an impact on other living beings—trees, birds, insects, mammals, and others—which may rely on them as sources of food or nutrients of another sort. Their annual life cycles are interesting to watch and the ways in which they cope with the conditions

around them are endlessly intriguing. This book is intended simply as an introduction to the world of wildflowers, but the interested reader is encouraged to go well beyond its pages and into nature itself, armed with any one of the excellent field guides that are available to help in identifying the thousands of different species that exist in North America.

Most of the flowers you will find have common names, such as passionflower or purple trillium, and these are usually descriptive in some way. (The passionflower is so named because certain parts of it relate to aspects of the story of the Crucifixion; the purple trillium because the flower is purple in color and has three distinct petals.) Nevertheless, in most field guides and in this book, you will find that each flower also has a name in Latin, its scientific name, since common names vary from region to region. The scarlet gilia, for instance, means one flower in the eastern United States (*Ipomopsis rubra*) and another species in the west (*Ipomopsis aggregata*); both flowers are members of the same phlox family, but they are different. The eastern flower grows along riverbanks, while the western flower favors dry slopes; the former is also known as standing cypress or Spanish larkspur in certain areas of Florida, while the latter is most commonly called skyrocket, though its unpleasant aroma causes the nickname skunk flower in many places. To complicate matters even further, neither flower is a true gilia. The use of scientific names, therefore, is very helpful in keeping order in the plant kingdom, just as it does in the animal world.

The naming system used for wildflowers is based on one devised by the Swedish botanist Carl Linnaeus, who selected Latin as a language that all educated people in the world would know; it also has the advantage of being a "dead" language that remains unchanged by daily usage (Greek words are also used in this system when necessary). The first word in the scientific name refers to the plant's genus—a group of closely related flowers within a family— and the second word is the species name. These words, like the common names, are often descriptive, too; the desert paintbrush (*Castilleja chromosa*) is named in honor of a Spanish botanist, Domingo Castillejo, and is very bright in color, for which the Greek word is *chroma*.

Being able to identify wildflowers accurately is very satisfying, but be sure not to overlook some of the other aspects of the flower as you observe it in nature. Look at the conditions in which it is growing—heavy shade or full sunlight, rich or sandy soil—and take note of the time of year during which the plant is blooming and the other plants that are growing in the vicinity. Keep in mind, for instance, that certain forest flowers bloom in the very early spring before the leaves of the trees above have blocked out the sunshine, while flowers that grow in fields often bloom much later in the summer. Note also the structure of the flower and try to determine the means by which it is pollinated and the way in which its seeds are dispersed. If you keep records of these observations, you might be able to use them in planting your own wildflower garden by reproducing or simulating the growing conditions where you live so that the plants will thrive much closer to your own home. Whether you choose to cultivate your own wildflowers or not, however, you will have learned something about the remarkable nature of these not-so-fragile blossoms and you will certainly have increased your own appreciation for the complexity and beauty of the natural world around you.

DESERT WILDFLOWERS

Desert Marigold
(*Baileya multiradiata;* see page 24.)
Murl Deusing

Deserts—those dry, inhospitable regions of the world—seem to be unlikely spots in which to find flowers, and it is true that deserts for much of the year are relatively bleak and colorless. But when the rains do come, the desert can erupt in glorious color, for it is during those brief periods that desert plants produce the seeds that will ensure their survival through the drought that inevitably follows. Desert annuals, which must complete a full cycle within the growing season—growing from seed to flower within a matter of weeks—escape the drought altogether, and their seeds may not germinate for years but remain in the soil waiting until the growing conditions are right. When they do bloom, they often do so in profusion, though the blossoms do not last long. Perennial plants last from year to year, but they must make special adaptations to cope with the drought, remaining dormant during the dry season or storing water in their leaves or stems, and flowering only when conditions are suitable.

PLAINS PRICKLYPEAR (*Opuntia polyacantha*)

Members of the cactus family have developed several ways of dealing with the arid conditions of our American deserts in the west and southwest. Like other succulent plants, they have shallow but extensive root systems that gather moisture from dew or from brief rain showers. They then store this water in their thick stems. They have few, if any, leaves but are usually equipped with spiny thorns that serve several purposes—to keep animals from eating the stems and fruit, to provide shade, and to reflect light and heat and thereby keep the plant cool. These plants absorb carbon dioxide during the night through pores in the skin of their

Plains Pricklypear (*Opuntia polyacantha*)
Richard Jepperson

21

stems, using it during the day for the process of photosynthesis, by which energy in plants is converted into carbohydrates. Pricklypears have flat, jointed stems and produce berrylike fruits that contain many seeds; some grow as trees or bushes, while others remain in low clumps. The plains pricklypear illustrated here is a low-growing bush with especially long, rigid spines that can create a nuisance for ranchers whose livestock try to eat it. It has a bright yellow or magenta flower, which will bloom from May to July, depending on rainfall.

PARRY'S CENTURY PLANT *(Agave parryi)*

Although the century plant may take many years to flower, it does not take a century! The flowers are well worth the wait, though. The plant is native to the deserts of the southwestern United States, and its Mexican relative is the well-known source of a juice that can be used to make the potent liquors mescal, tequila, and pulque. Indians have also used this plant as a source of drink, food, medicine, and the materials with which they make fiber and weapons. Century plants are members of the amaryllis family, which also boasts daffodils and jonquils as well as the cultivated amaryllis. Like the cactus, they are succulents, storing moisture in their leaves, which are very sharp, with spines at the tip and along the sides. The flowers, which may appear between June and September, grow on a tall stalk in clusters that face upward.

OCOTILLO *(Fouquieria splendens)*

This unusual plant, the only one of its family to exist in North America, is also covered with spines on the stems like the cactus. It is not a succulent, however, and does not store water. Instead, it has developed the ability to avoid losing water by simply dropping its leaves during the dry season and growing them quickly after each rainfall. Like the leaves, the bright red flowers, which grow at the top of the tall stems, may appear several times a year during the

Parry's Century Plant *(Agave parryi)*
Robert Dunne

Ocotillo
(*Fouquieria splendens*)
F. Gohier

Sego Lily (*Calochortus nuttallii*)
Bob & Elsie Boggs

INDIAN OR DESERT PAINTBRUSH
(*Castilleja chromosa*)

There are several similar-looking members of the group of flowers, most of which are native to the west (the Indian paintbrush *Castilleja coccinea* is the only species known in the east). They are well named, for the brightly colored bracts (which are leaves, not flowers) look as if they have been dipped in bright red paint. The flowers themselves are inconspicuous green-yellow tubular blooms inside the bracts. Indian paintbrushes are often considered parasites—or at least partial parasites—for their roots can connect with the root systems of other plants, usually grasses. This is an effective method of tapping into a water supply when this precious commodity is at a real premium. Paintbrushes are annuals or biennials, and when they bloom in profusion they make a spectacular show, which is why they are called "prairie fire" in some locations.

DESERT MARIGOLD (*Baileya multiradiata*)

These brilliant yellow flowers are commonly seen along the road in deserts of the southwest, where they grow in thick patches, often extending for miles. They are related to asters and daisies and are frequently cultivated in gardens, where their flowers will bloom all summer long. When desert rains have been generous in winter, these marigolds are joined by other brightly colored flowers, such as blue lupines and red globemallows, to create a wonderful display in the flat, arid Arizona desert.

warm season. Indians and other desert people have found many uses for this plant: food, firewood, fences, leather conditioning, and medication, for the root when powdered is supposed to reduce inflammation.

SEGO LILY (*Calochortus nuttallii*)

There are several members of the lily family that live in arid regions—the mariposa tulips, mojave yucca, and this pretty white flower, which is found on the plains and in open pine forests of the west and midwest. One of the reasons lilies can handle the dry desert climate is that they form bulbs or rhizomes in which the plant can remain dormant for long periods of time underground. The sego lily can be seen in bloom from May to July, depending on its location, and its bell-shaped flowers grow at the top of erect stems which bear only a few leaves. This is the state flower of Utah, for it was the Ute Indians who showed the Mormon settlers of the state how the bulb made a nutritious food when other foods were scarce.

Indian or Desert Paintbrush
(Castilleja chromosa)
Joe DiStefano

FIELD WILDFLOWERS

Passionflower
(*Passiflora incarnata*; see page 39.)
Ken Brate

In the days before North America was settled by Europeans, natural grasslands spread for miles in the central part of the continent, supporting enormous herds of grazing animals. Those vast prairies or plains still exist but are now mostly cultivated with "amber waves of grain" rather than the wild grasses that once thrived there, and domestic livestock have largely replaced the wild bison. Nevertheless, some of the original character of the natural grassland has remained, since the climate is unchanged and the land is still dominated by grassy plants rather than trees requiring greater rainfall to survive. The winters are very cold there and the summers hot and dry because the prairies are open to the drying winds that sweep through, unbroken by trees or mountains, and so the plants that are native to the re-

gion have adapted to the special conditions that prevail. Many of the major plants have deep roots that grow to fifteen feet or more in search of water and nutrients; many of them are pollinated by the wind. This explains why grasses, for instance, have such inconspicuous flowers, as they do not need to attract insects. Even the insect-pollinated wildflowers take advantage of the wind, for many of them use it to disperse their seeds. A number of the flowers are annual or biennial, growing new plants from seed every year or two, but several are perennials, withstanding the cold and drought beneath the earth in bulbs, corms, or rhizomes.

Elsewhere on the continent fields are common, but most of these are considered artificial, since they have been created by cutting down trees to provide meadows for farming, pastures for grazing livestock, or lawns. Although these fields are often rich in wildflowers, many of the flowers have migrated from the midwestern grasslands and adapted to

California Poppy (*Eschscholtzia californica*; see page 38.)
Tom McHugh

27

Black-eyed Susan
(*Rudbeckia hirta*)
Louise K. Broman

treeless areas elsewhere, often at the expense of being considered weeds.

Natural meadows, such as those in the west and along the coast in the east and south, including the great savannahs in South Carolina and Georgia, are also relatively treeless, like the Great Plains, but they are usually blessed with heavier rainfall than the Great Plains and one may find any number of unusual wildflowers there that cannot be seen elsewhere on the continent.

COMMON SUNFLOWER (*Helianthus annuus*)

This impressive flower is perhaps one of the most characteristic of all field flowers, a common sight in fields throughout the continent. It is a member of the composite or sunflower family, which contains as many as nineteen thousand species worldwide, including such popular flowers as the daisy, zinnia, dahlia, aster, and such weedy varieties as ragweed, goldenrod, yarrow, and dandelion, as well as

Common Sunflower (*Helianthus annuus*)
Harold W. Hoffman

useful vegetables like the Jerusalem artichoke and lettuce. Although the sunflower, like the daisy and aster, appears to produce a single blossom, the actual flowers are quite small, arranged in heads that contain two different types of flower—the disk flowers in the center and the large petal-like ray flowers around the edge. The seeds, which have a relatively hard shell, are produced by the disk flowers and are often of great use to animals and man. Indians once made bread from sunflower-seed flour and used the oil for various purposes; sunflower seeds are a staple for many species of birds and are considered a delicacy for humans. There are about sixty native species of sunflower, including the giant sunflower (which may grow to twelve feet in height) and a cultivated variety which has an exceptionally large flower head. The common sunflower is the state flower of Kansas, though it also grows in many other areas.

BLACK-EYED SUSAN (*Rudbeckia hirta*)

This handsome flower, the state flower of Maryland, is clearly a relative of the sunflower, with its brown disk flowers and yellow rays, but it is distinctive in several ways. It is a member of a group called coneflowers, because the central disk flowers grow in a cone shape; the ray flowers tend to slope downward rather than extend horizontally as in the sunflowers. This is a biennial plant (the sunflower is an annual), producing only leaves in its first year and flowers the next. It grows a tall stem like the sunflower but its leaves are covered with hair that makes them furry to the touch.

BUSHY ASTER (Aster dumosus)

There are as many as 150 species of aster native to North America, and they too are clearly relatives of the sunflower,

although the colors of their ray flowers are most often blue, lavender, or white rather than yellow, and they are not usually as tall. The bushy aster illustrated here rarely exceeds three feet and it is most common in the south, though it is also found near the Great Lakes. Most asters are typical field flowers, though some grow in swamps, woods, and along the shore. Some members of the aster group have very large, showy flowers and these are sometimes grown commercially. Most asters, which are also known as Michaelmas daisies, are perennials and have adapted to areas where they have become plentiful enough to be considered weeds, especially in the northeast.

ROUGH-STEMMED GOLDENROD (Solidago rugosa)

This colorful wildflower, which is especially abundant in the northeast, is also commonly considered a weed, not only because it grows in large masses in hayfields to the consternation of farmers but also because it has been blamed for causing hay fever during the late summer when it blooms. (Actually, the offending plant is ragweed, which produces its irritating pollen at the same time as goldenrod.) In earlier days, doctors thought that goldenrod actually had healing powers, though this, too, seems to be only a rumor. There are many different species of goldenrod and some of them grow in marshes and deserts as well as fields, but they share many characteristics with other members of the sunflower family of which they are a member. They grow fairly high (up to four feet or so) and have lance-shaped leaves with long stalks and tiny flowers that grow in heads. Goldenrods are perennial plants and lose their stalks each fall, growing from the roots in spring; they are pollinated by wind and their seeds are dispersed the same way, being neatly equipped with seed parachutes that carry them some distance.

PRAIRIE BLAZING STAR (Liatris pycnostachya)

These pretty lavender flowers do not much resemble sunflowers, but they are relatives with a similar flower struc-

Bushy Aster (Aster dumosus)
Mary M. Thacher

Rough-stemmed Goldenrod
(Solidago rugosa)
Peter G. Aitken

Pennsylvania Smartweed
(*Polygonum pensylvanicum*)
Pat Lynch

Prairie Blazing Star
(*Liatris pycnostachya*)
Tom Evans

ture—heads made up of disk flowers, minus only the distinctive ray flowers. As the name implies, these flowers are found on the midwestern prairies, although some of the other blazing stars grow in the northeast and south as well. Some species, including this one, are grown as ornamental garden flowers.

SWEET JOE-PYE WEED (*Eupatorium purpureum*)

Like the blazing stars, the various species of Joe-Pye weed (named for a New England Indian doctor who used the plant to cure ailments) grow clusters of flowers on a tall sturdy stem. Boneset, a closely related plant, has also had medicinal uses in the past; its name comes from the fact that early physicians used its leaves in bandaging fractures, assuming that the shape of the plant indicated its special properties as a splint. Sweet Joe-Pye weed also gets its name from the fact that the leaves give off a vanillalike aroma

when broken. Like other flowers in the composite family, the seeds are dispersed by wind in tiny parachutes, which has enabled the plant to spread widely throughout the eastern half of the United States.

PENNSYLVANIA SMARTWEED (*Polygonum pensylvanicum*)

Although this plant may resemble the Joe-Pye weed, it is actually in a different family, the buckwheat group, which also contains rhubarb. There are nearly thirty smartweed species, which are distinguished by their tiny petalless flowers that grow in dense clusters on tall spikelike stems. The name comes from the fact that the plant produces a juice that is quite pungent and will cause the eyes to water. Although the plant is considered a weed in some cultivated areas, its seeds are an important source of food for wild birds.

Sweet Joe-Pye Weed
(*Eupatorium purpureum*; see page 33.)
Parker

Farewell to Spring (*Clarkia amoena*)
Farrell Grehan

FEW-FLOWERED SHOOTING STAR
(*Dodecatheon pulchellum*)

Most of the field flowers we have seen so far have been native to the midwest or eastern half of the continent, but this flower is found on the coastal prairies west of the Rocky Mountains. There are several other species of shooting star, members of the primrose family, and they all share the same flower structure, with dart-shaped blossoms that seem to point in all directions from the central stalk. Some shooting stars are cultivated as garden flowers, but all are pollinated by bees who are attracted to the color and the nectar. The word *primrose* comes from the Latin word for "first," since flowers in this family are among the first to bloom in springtime.

EVENING PRIMROSE (*Oenothera biennis*)

Although this flower does, true to its name, bloom at night,

Few-flowered Shooting Star (*Dodecatheon pulchellum*)
Alford W. Cooper

Texas Bluebonnet (*Lupinus subcarnosus*; see page 38.)
Russ Kinne

it is not a true primrose but an unrelated plant which apparently reminded European settlers of wild primroses back home. Its bright yellow color and sweet lemony fragrance enable the night-flying insects that pollinate the plant to find it in the dark. As its species name implies, the plant is a biennial, growing leaves during the first year and flowering late in the following year. Birds thrive on its seeds, and hungry humans have found its roots edible and nourishing.

FAREWELL TO SPRING (*Clarkia amoena*)

This lovely member of the evening primrose family is a western flower; its genus name *Clarkia*, in fact, was given in honor of Captain Clark who with Lewis explored the northwest in the early nineteenth century. Like its relatives, it blooms at night during the midsummer months, when the temperature is bearable. Because these flowers are relatively restricted in territory, they are rare.

Evening Primrose (*Oenothera biennis*)
Tom Branch

TEXAS BLUEBONNET *(Lupinus subcarnosus)*

Like farewell to spring, which is restricted almost entirely to California, this flower is rarely seen outside Texas, for which it is the official state flower. Its small, dark blue flowers grow in an elongated cluster, and in springtime one may see fields full of the blossoms in the eastern and southern parts of the state. As the scientific name indicates, this flower is one of several lupine species, some of which are cultivated in gardens.

CALIFORNIA POPPY *(Eschscholtzia californica)*

This, too, is a state flower, and, interestingly enough, is often found blooming alongside a western lupine relative of the Texas bluebonnet, turning the fields of California a brilliant patchwork of blue and orange. A relative of the opium poppy, this flower has a spicy (but not narcotic) fragrance, which attracts the insects that pollinate it. It grows in fields along the foothills of the Rockies and in valleys of the Pacific coast and is often grown as a garden flower.

ELDERBERRY *(Sambucus canadensis)*

Another fragrant flower, this native of the eastern half of the continent is a member of the honeysuckle family, though its flowers are so tiny that it is difficult at first glance to make out the trumpet shape typical of the group. Although the elderberry is sometimes cultivated for its flowers, its primary interest for man has been its dark berrylike fruit, which is used in making jelly and wine.

WILD HYACINTH *(Camassia scilloides)*

This plant, too, has had its uses for humans, since its bulb was often used as food by Indians. It is a member of the lily family, which also includes the onion, and is similar in appearance to the cultivated hyacinths although it is not closely related. It is a spring flower, blooming in May and June in meadows in the east and west.

Wild Hyacinth (*Camassia scilloides*)
Anthony Bleeker, Jr.

Elderberry
(*Sambucus canadensis*)
Dr. Robt. H. Potts, Jr.

PASQUEFLOWER *(Anemone patens)*

This handsome flower of the northern midwest is the state flower of South Dakota. It is also known by a number of other names—wild crocus and blue tulip, because of its shape, and prairie anemone—but its most common name, pasqueflower, comes from the fact that it oftens blooms around Easter. Although noted for its purple or blue color, the flower has no petals at all but colorful sepals that surround the yellow stamens in a deep cup. After pollination, the flowers drop off, leaving clusters of seeds with long, feathery tails that can be carried for some distance in the wind. It is not until after the seeds are produced that leaves appear. Like many plants that must undergo difficult climate conditions (this flower is found on mountain slopes as well as in the windswept prairie), the pasqueflower has tiny hairs on the stems and sepals, giving it a fuzzy appearance and helping it to retain warmth.

PASSIONFLOWER *(Passiflora incarnata)*

Another flower named for Easter, this plant is a member of a tropical family, though it is widely seen in the southern United States. Its name comes from the fact that parts of the flower seem to bear a relationship to the story of the Crucifixion, complete with a crown of thorns, nails (which are actually the stigmas), wounds (the stamens), and ten of the disciples (five sepals and five petals).

Fringed Gentian
(*Gentiana crinita*)
Louise K. Broman

FRINGED GENTIAN *(Gentiana crinita)*

An increasingly rare species is the beautiful fringed gentian with its distinctive blue flower, which blooms late in the summer or early in fall. It is a biennial, blooming in its second year, and it grows in the northeast where it is among the last wildflowers to appear in the season. Gentian roots have been used to produce a medicinal tonic; in fact, the name gentian comes from that of an ancient king who is supposed to have discovered the medical uses of the plant. The word *fringed* refers to the delicate structure of the petal, which is designed to collapse at the slightest touch and thus prevent crawling insects from disturbing the flower. Although usually seen in open areas, the fringed gentian is also considered a woodland flower, for it can be found along the edges of forests.

Pasqueflower
(*Anemone patens*; see page 39.)
S. J. Krasemann

WETLAND WILDFLOWERS

Golden Ragwort
(*Senecio aureus*; see page 48.)
Ken Brate

Water is essential to life, and for many plants and animals that means fresh water as it falls to earth in the form of rain or as it collects in inland ponds and lakes (which are themselves connected by streams and rivers). The wetlands alongside these bodies of water are rich in wildlife, and though the average human regards these swampy areas as unusable nuisances, they are an integral part of what scientists call "ecological succession," by which the land evolves from one type of habitat to another. For example, as ponds and lakes become filled with vegetation, their depth is decreased until they reach the swamp stage, an important breeding place for birds, insects, and other animals. Gradually, these swamps build up earth, thanks to the decaying

vegetation, and become marshes, which resemble wet meadows and are especially rich in wildflowers, small mammals, birds, and even more insects. In due course, that marsh will become bog and then meadow, which will support tree life and eventually become forest.

All of this changing, of course, takes thousands of years when nature is directing the activity; unfortunately, humans have learned to speed up and alter the process, filling in bodies of water and swamplands to construct buildings, destroying natural habitats as they go. As a result, many animals and plants have become increasingly rare as they have fewer places in which to live. In this chapter, we will take a closer look at some of the different wildflowers that prefer a wetland environment, and it should quickly become clear just how desirable these areas are, if only because of the variety and richness of the life they support.

Fragrant Water Lily (*Nymphaea odorata*; see page 44.)
Richard H. Smith

FRAGRANT WATER LILY *(Nymphaea odorata)*

There are about seventy species of water lilies throughout the world, but this is one of the most common North American water lilies. Native to the eastern half of the continent it has adapted to life in western ponds as well. It is an aquatic plant, living entirely in water, with extremely long stems that extend into the mud on the pond's bottom. The broad floating leaves have a waxy surface so that the

water will roll off, but they also have an unusual adaptation to a watery life—pores in the leaves that absorb carbon dioxide are located on the upper surface rather than on the underside of the leaf, where they appear in most land plants. The flowers, too, float on the surface, and they give off a pleasant aroma during the mornings when they are open, which attracts insects to pollinate them.

ARROWHEAD *(Sagittaria Latifolia)*

This aquatic plant, a member of the water plantain family, also grows in water, burying its roots deep in the muddy bottom. Early in the spring, underwater leaves appear and eventually these are followed by another set of leaves, which are oval and float on the surface. Finally, the arrow-shaped leaves for which the plant is named appear in the air above. The plant also produces two types of flowers, male and female, and these can be distinguished because the latter do not have any of the distinctive white petals. The plant's rhizomes, which remain in the muck beneath the water, are edible; ducks and muskrats eat them as is, while the Algonquin Indians used to roast them like potatoes.

WATER HYACINTH *(Eichhornia crassipes)*

Like other members of the pickerelweed family, the water hyacinth is an aquatic plant and it has a cluster of pretty blue-violet flowers that grow on a spikelike stem. Its leaves contain pockets of air that help it to float in water and it is a very hardy plant indeed, much to the dismay of humans who use the southern waterways where it has become a weed. It is not a native plant but was introduced from the tropics, and millions of dollars have been spent trying to remove it from rivers where it has become severely overgrown. It is thought, however, that the plant might have some beneficial effect on the environment where waters have become polluted. Since it absorbs nutrients from the water it may, if harvested periodically, be used to remove toxic elements.

Buttonbush *(Cephalanthus occidentalis)*
James H. Carmichael, Jr.

BUTTONBUSH (Cephalanthus occidentalis)

This pretty little flower, a member of the bedstraw family that also contains the cultivated gardenia, grows alongside ponds and streams and in swamps, where it can withstand the occasional floods that can kill off other plants that are not so readily adapted to an aquatic life. Its range is the eastern half of the continent, and it can reach a height of ten feet where conditions require it. Ducks and other wildlife are very fond of the fruit heads produced by the small, ball-like flowers.

Arrowhead (*Sagittaria iatifolia*)   A. W. Ambler

Water Hyacinth
(*Eichhornia crassipes*)
Robert C. Hermes

Pussy Willow
(*Salix discolor*)
George & Judy Manna

CATTAIL (*Typha latifolia*)

A characteristic sight in marshes throughout the world is the sausage-shaped spike of the cattail which grows in shallow water, often in great numbers. Although most people do not think of it as a wildflower, the brown cylinder is in fact a flower head consisting of many tiny female flowers without petals. The male flowers bloom for a shorter period; these appear as a spike of fluffy yellow flowers above the female cylinder and fall off after pollination has taken place. This plant spreads by means of creeping rootstocks, which are starchy and edible and have been used as food by both humans and animals. The leaves are a favorite food of certain insects, and other sections of the plant—including the flower spikes—can be boiled and eaten with some pleasure.

PUSSY WILLOW (*Salix discolor*)

Another plant that is rarely thought of as a wildflower is this attractive member of the willow family, which in many areas signals the arrival of spring by producing furry catkins even before it produces leaves. Like the cattail, the pussy-willow flowers are easily distinguished by sex: the male catkins have yellow stamens, while the females are greenish and appear on separate plants. Pussy willows range widely through Canada, the northeast, and in the midwest, growing along streams and in swampy areas.

Cardinal flower (*Lobelia cardinalis*; see page 48.)
Pat Lynch

Cattails
(*Typha latifolia*)
Robert J. Ashworth

Hibiscus (*Hibiscus coccineus*)
Peter Fink

Scarlet Gilia (*Ipomopsis rubra*)
Ken Brate

CARDINAL FLOWER (*Lobelia cardinalis*)

Another streamside flower is the beautiful cardinal flower, the only red member of the bluebell family. It is so lovely in fact that many people grow the flower as an ornamental and others, unfortunately, pick it where it grows in the wild, so that it has become rare in some areas. The inch-long tubular flowers formed by the stamens that grow around the style are usually pollinated by hummingbirds, who are attracted to the color and are capable of reaching down the relatively long tube with their beaks.

SCARLET GILIA (*Ipomopsis rubra*)

This plant, too, produces tubular red flowers and is often cultivated in gardens but it is not related to the cardinal flower; instead, it is a member of the phlox family. It grows along riverbanks, unlike its close relative the scarlet gilia or skyrocket of the west (*Ipomopsis aggregata*), which is also nicknamed the skunk flower, as it has a slightly skunky odor in the leaves, which may attract certain pollinating insects.

GOLDEN RAGWORT (*Senecio aureus*)

Lest you think that all flowers in the composite or sunflower family live in fields, let us examine the pretty golden ragwort, which prefers swamps and damp meadows. It looks very much like a daisy with yellow disk and ray flowers, and it is found throughout the east and midwest. It is closely related to a group of composites known as groundsels, which inhabit open prairies, but, unlike them and other grasslands flowers, it tends to bloom earlier in the spring.

HIBISCUS (*Hibiscus coccineus*)

This lovely red flower is part of the mallow family, which also includes hollyhocks, rose of Sharon, and other, more tropical hibiscus flowers, as well as the edible okra and the cotton plants. Although some of the western hibiscus plants can be found in arid desert regions, this southern species prefers marshes and swamps, though it is sometimes

Spider Lily (*Hymenocallis liriosme*; see page 50.)
Maude Dorr

48

cultivated in gardens. In certain areas the plant may grow as high as ten feet and the blossoms may reach a width of eight inches, making it one of our most impressive wildflowers.

SPIDER LILY (Hymenocallis liriosme)

This is another southern flower that likes watery marshes. It is not a true lily but a member of the amaryllis family, like the Easter lily and the century plant. What is distinctive about this flower is its cuplike formation, which contains the stamens, and its six long white petals (three of which are actually petallike sepals), which give it a spidery appearance.

BLUE FLAG (Iris versicolor)

This handsome violet flower is a familiar sight in wetlands of the northeast (there is a similar species, the southern blue flag, which is found in the southeast). It is pollinated by insects, which must make their way through the flower's complicated structure to do the job. The large violet-and-yellow petals are actually sepals; the three petals are violet and stand upright, while the three styles arch over them, hiding the stamens beneath them. Like its cousins the crocus, gladiolus, and cultivated iris, the blue flag is a perennial, spending the cold months of the year underground in the form of a rhizome and growing new stalks and leaves every spring.

Jack-in-the-pulpit (*Arisaema triphyllum*)
Robert Dunne

Blue Flag (*Iris versicolor*)
Lincoln Nutting

TRUMPETS *(Sarracenia flava)*

The complicated structure of this plant also poses a problem for insects, but of a much different kind, for this is a carnivorous plant which feeds on the insects that drown in the water collected in its hollow leaves. Like other members of the pitcher-plant family, the trumpets live in bogs and are becoming increasingly rare, probably because they are collected as curiosities. This flower has a distinctive odor that attracts the insects, which then fall into the pitcher-shaped leaf structure and drown, to be digested by the plant.

JACK-IN-THE-PULPIT *(Arisaema triphyllum)*

Another interestingly contructed plant is this member of the arum family, which also includes the taro plant and skunk cabbage, and a number of houseplants, such as philodendron and dieffenbachia. It inhabits swamps and wet woodlands of the east and once served as a food for Indians, who cooked the roots, giving the plant its other common name of Indian turnip. The name jack-in-the-pulpit is descriptive of the plant's appearance: the pulpit is a hood of green or dark brown bracts that encloses a "jack," or cylindrical structure called the spadix. At the base of the spadix grow the reproductive organs, tiny male and female flowers that eventually produce shiny red berries in the fall.

JEWELWEED *(Impatiens capensis)*

Like jack-in-the-pulpit, this interesting orange flower prefers wetlands with trees to shade it; a relative of the cultivated impatiens, it has succulent stems that contain a juice with fungicidal properties. The other common name for this plant is spotted touch-me-not, since the mechanism that releases the seeds is very sensitive to the touch when the fruit is ripe. As the fruit, or pod, ripens, it forms segments that are joined at the tip; when these are touched, the segments curl up and hurl out the seeds, often for a considerable distance. This flower is pollinated by hummingbirds as well as insects and is an annual that often grows in large patches.

Trumpets (*Sarracenia flava*)
Y. Momatiuk

Purple Gerardia
(*Agalinis purpurea*)
Sturgis McKeever

PURPLE GERARDIA *(Agalinis purpurea)*

Another colorful flower that likes a moist habitat is this close relative of the foxglove group. The dainty pink flowers are bell-shaped, with tubular corollas formed by five fused petals, and the plant has many branches with relatively small leaves. It is an annual plant that spreads widely via its seeds, which are contained in a berry.

WHITE FRINGED ORCHID
(Habenaria blephariglottis)

Although most members of the large, fascinating orchid family are native to the tropics, there are many species that

Jewelweed (*Impatiens capensis;* see page 51.)
Constance Porter

grow wild in North America. This lovely flower is found in wet meadows and marshes throughout the east, from Newfoundland to Florida. Orchids are perennial plants, and their flowers are complex structures with three true petals, the lowest of which has a liplike shape. The flowers of the white fringed orchid plant grow in clusters, and the lip petal has a pronounced fringe, hence the name. They bloom during the summer months and are pollinated by moths.

GLADES MORNING GLORY *(Ipomoea sagittata)*

This flower is not a freshwater plant but prefers the brackish soil of the southern coastlines. Like the other morning glories, it is a vine that produces funnel-shaped flowers and it is very showy indeed. Because it inhabits a southern environment, it blooms all year round. Its leaves are very sim-

ilar in appearance to that of the aquatic arrowroot, which shares the same species name, *sagittata*, from the Latin word for "arrow."

VENUS FLYTRAP *(Dionaea muscipula)*

Another coastal plant is this fascinating carnivorous flower, which is restricted in range to wet sandy plains of North and South Carolina. Like the trumpets it has developed an especially effective way to obtain nutrients that cannot be found in the soil, but it is rather more aggressive in the way it goes about its predatory task. The red leaf resembles a flower and this, together with the sweet nectar, attracts insects. When an insect or spider happens to move across the hairs on the upper surface of the leaf, the "jaws" of the leaf snap shut, trapping the victim inside. It may take the plant several days to digest the insect, after which time the leaf opens up in readiness for another meal. Each leaf lasts long enough to catch food three times and then it drops off. This intriguing plant is very rare, not only because of its restricted habitat but also because it has been collected as a curiosity, like the trumpets.

White Fringed Orchid *(Habenaria blephariglottis;* see page 53.)
Sturgis McKeever

Bird-foot Violet
(*Viola pedata*)
J. L. Lepore

blossom and usually blooms in May throughout the eastern half of the continent. It inhabits thick woods and shady clearings; this may explain the enormous size of the leaves, which must gather as much sunlight as possible in order to photosynthesize. The flower itself is relatively small and solitary, growing between a pair of leaves, as if under an umbrella. Although the roots were once used for medicinal purposes by Indians, the roots, leaves, and seeds are toxic. The plant's other common name, mandrake, derives from the root's similarity to the mandrake of Europe.

Painted Trillium
(*Trillium undulatum*; see page 62.)
Frank. J. Miller

Wood Sorrel (*Oxalis montana*)
Angelina Lax

Bunchberry (*Cornus canadensis*)
Steve Coombs

WOOD SORREL *(Oxalis montana)*

Most members of the wood sorrel family are tropical plants but there are a few native species, including this pretty flower that likes the wooded hills and mountains of the east. Some wood sorrels are considered weeds, because they spread rapidly by runners from the bulb and are difficult to eradicate. A few are cultivated for their flowers, and a number of them are grown for their leaves, which have a distinctly sour taste. The common sourgrass plant is actually a European introduction, but all wood sorrels have the same sour flavor, hence the genus name *Oxalis*, from the Greek word for "sour." The wood sorrel illustrated is not easily cultivated but is a common wildflower in its range.

BUNCHBERRY *(Cornus canadensis)*

This northern plant is distinguished as one of only two species in the dogwood family to be an herb rather than a full tree. It likes cool climate and can be found in southern Canada as well as in the northern United States, blooming from May to midsummer. Although it looks like a simple flower within a ring of six leaves, it is actually a complex structure, made up of four petallike bracts that surround many tiny yellow flowers. By autumn these flowers have given way to clusters of bright red berries (hence the plant's name). This plant is cultivated in some areas as a ground cover.

WILD GERANIUM *(Geranium maculatum)*

It is not surprising that this plant does not resemble the familiar potted geranium, for they are not closely related; the cultivated variety derives from a South African genus. Wild geraniums can be found in the east and west, some of them called cranesbills and regarded as weeds that are especially abundant on lawns and in gardens. This species likes the relatively cool woods of the northeast and midwest and blooms in May, later producing seeds, which birds will help disperse to form next year's wild geranium crop.

Wild Geranium
(*Geranium maculatum*)
V. Crich

SMOOTH SOLOMON'S SEAL
(*Polygonatum biflorum*)

Another May-June flower is this pretty member of the lily family, which somewhat resembles the cultivated lily-of-the-valley, with its white bell-like flowers drooping from an arched stem. Like many other lilies, the plant is a perennial, its stalk emerging each spring from an underground stem, or rhizome, which was a staple food for Indians and early settlers. The scar formed when a leaf stalk is removed from the rhizome is apparently shaped like the official seal of King Solomon, which is what gives the plant its name. This woodland plant has relatively large light green leaves that frequently hide the flowers, which eventually ripen into dark blue berries.

Smooth Solomon's Seal (*Polygonatum biflorum*)
Ken Brate

MOUNTAIN LAUREL *(Kalmia latifolia)*

This relative of the trailing arbutus is actually a shrub that can grow to a height of fifteen feet or more and which may live many years. The evergreen leaves are an attractive shiny green and the flowers, which bloom in early summer, grow in beautiful clusters of pink or white. The flowers mature gradually so that you can often see buds and open flowers on the same bush; the insects that feed on the nectar will sometimes cause the stamen to pop up out of the bud. The state flower of Connecticut, the mountain laurel is often grown as an ornamental in shady areas, for it prefers open woods and can be found over much of the east and south.

PINK LADY'S SLIPPER *(Cypripedium acaule)*

There are more than twenty thousand species of orchids worldwide and most of them are native to the tropical rain-forest regions of the world. However, there are at least a hundred orchids native to North America, and one of the most commonly seen is the lady's slipper, which prefers forested areas of the northern United States and southern Canada. There are several species; the one illustrated is from the east, where it likes pine woods and can be found at high elevations in rocky areas. Most orchids are prized for their distinctive shapes and colors; the lady's slipper is no exception, with its inflated slipperlike petal called a lip. This pouch is constructed so that insects must make their way past the stigma, where they deposit pollen from another flower, and then under the anthers where they pick up fresh pollen. Like all orchids, lady's slippers are difficult to cultivate and should never be picked.

WILD COLUMBINE *(Aquilegia canadensis)*

Columbines are in the buttercup family and are among our loveliest woodland flowers, which can often be found in mountain meadows, especially in the west, as well as in open woods, and in many gardens throughout the country. The blue columbine of the west is the state flower of Colorado and is especially handsome with five blue sepals sup-

Wild Columbine (*Aquilegia canadensis*)
John Serrao

Pink Lady's Slipper
(*Cypripedium acaule*)
Mary Ann D'Esopo

Showy Tick Trefoil
(*Desmodium canadense*)
Richard Parker

porting five white petals with yellowish stamens in the center. The wild columbine illustrated here is found east of the Rockies and is red and yellow in color, with yellow stamens visible as they hang below the yellow and red petals and red sepals. The tubular shape of the flowers must be pollinated by long-tongued insects such as bees which are attracted to the sweet nectar.

GAYWINGS *(Polygala paucifolia)*

This intriguing-looking pink flower, which resembles a tiny airplane or even a butterfly, looks as if it should belong to the orchid family, but actually it is a milkwort that prefers the rich woods of the northeast and the mountains of the south. Milkworts that grow in open areas of the southeast tend to bloom relatively late in the season, but this one—presumably because it must cope with dense overhead leaves—blooms as early as May in some regions. The name milkwort derives from the old belief that the consumption of these plants would stimulate milk production in cows or humans (the Greek word *polygala* means "much milk").

BEE BALM *(Monarda didyma)*

This aromatic member of the mint family is often cultivated for its flowers but it was once grown for its leaves, which were used by Indians and early colonists to make tea, hence its other common name, Oswego tea, named for the Oswego Indians of New York State. Like the wild columbine, it has red tubular flowers, but these grow in a cluster atop a stem rather than singly on tall stalks. Hummingbirds are attracted to these flowers, presumably because of the red color and the fragrance. Bee balm flowers relatively late in the summer for a woodland species, another reason for its popularity in the garden.

SHOWY TICK TREFOIL *(Desmodium canadense)*

If you have ever walked through the woods or fields of the east and midwest in late summer and come back covered with flat, fuzzy seeds, you have probably already met one of the tick trefoil plants, also known as sticktights, tickclovers, and beggarweeds. These are seedpod segments that break off from the plant and attach themselves to animal fur and clothing, which ensures seed dispersal. The prettiest wildflower in the group is the one illustrated here with its pink clustered, pealike flowers (not surprising, since the plant is in the pea family), which grow on elongated stalks.

Bee Balm *(Monarda didyma)*
Peter G. Aitkin

Indian Pipe
(*Monotropa uniflora*)
H. A. Thornhill

INDIAN PIPE (Monotropa uniflora)

As we have seen, most woodland plants cope with decreased sunlight under the heavy leaf canopy of the midsummer forest by blooming early in the spring or by growing in relatively open areas, but this curious plant has adapted to its sunless habitat in a very different way, so that it can flower as late as September even in the deep woods. It has no chlorophyll at all and thus is completely white rather than green, and it obtains all of its nutrients from the forest floor rather than through leaves. Thanks to a certain type of fungus, with which the Indian pipe has developed a mutual bond, the plant can parasitize the roots of living plants or feed on decaying vegetation. It produces a solitary flower, which droops from the thick translucent stem, and has tiny scalelike leaves that appear on the stalk. As the fruit ripens, the flower becomes erect, but after the seeds disperse—or if the flower is picked—the plant turns black. Some orchids share this same system of obtaining nutrients, but the Indian pipe is actually a member of the heath family, as is the blueberry and the rhododendron.

SNOW PLANT (Sarcodes sanguinea)

Equally unusual, though perhaps more attractive because of its bright red color, is this intriguing member of the wintergreen family. It can be found in the coniferous forests of the west coast from Oregon to California. Like the Indian pipe, it has no green at all and its leaves are simply scalelike formations on the stem, which supports a number of bell-shaped flowers. Also like the Indian pipe, the snow plant is a saphrophyte, deriving all of its nutrients from the rich humus produced by layers and layers of decaying vegetation, thanks to its relationship with fungi.

Unlike the deciduous forest, the coniferous forest produces leaves that are decay-resistant, so that it takes many years for the humus to develop; the soil itself is relatively poor and acidic, having been combed away by the glaciers, and the winters are cold and long (although the snow does serve to protect the forest floor and the plants within it). It is not surprising that we find few wildflowers in this environment or that the ones we do see have a very special nature, like the Indian pipe and the snow plant.

Snow Plant (*Sarcodes sanguinea*)
Al Lowry

ALPINE WILDFLOWERS

Purple Saxifrage
(*Saxifraga oppositifolia*)
Barry Griffiths

A mountain may contain a number of different habitats, ranging from rich woodland below to the colder, drier coniferous level above to the treeless alpine tundra at the top. The plants that can survive the extremely difficult conditions above the treeline are among the hardiest in existence. They tend to be slow-growing perennials that need not start a new plant each year during the very short growing season; they are low-growing and have roots that enable them to cling to the wind-swept rocks and store nutrients for the long winter. Even during the brief summer, they must withstand extreme shifts in temperature as the intense sun gives way to the chill of evening.

Plants of the tundra—the arctic region above the coniferous forest, or taiga, and below the area where ice is permanent year-round—share many of the same characteristics with alpine plants, for they too must cope with a short growing season and a treeless environment. Many of these plants do not produce flowers every year but develop slowly, putting their energy into their roots; yet when they do flower, they can be among the most exquisite of nature's productions. The temptation to pick them is great, but the reasons not to do so are many. Since they may bloom infrequently, one should give the blossoms a chance to help the plants survive when they do appear; also, many plants are unique to these mountain areas and can be found nowhere else.

PURPLE SAXIFRAGE (*Saxifraga oppositifolia*)

Many species in the saxifrage family can be found in woodlands, on prairies, and along streams, but most members of

Dwarf Cinquefoil (*Potentilla robbinsiana;* see page 77.)
Noble Proctor

Diapensia
(Diapensia lapponica)
Noble Proctor

Subalpine Buttercup
(*Ranunculus eschscholtzii*)
Pat & Tom Leeson

this hardy family prefer cooler regions. The purple saxifrage can be found in many places across Canada and the northern United States, where it grows on rocky cliffs or on ledges. Like many alpine or tundra plants, it is a low, densely growing plant with small leaves that are edged with small, stiff hairs that tend to retain warmth and protect the surface. The brightly colored flowers appear in the summer when the weather is at its most bearable. There are a number of mountain saxifrages that are unique to particular areas, including the starlike saxifrage of Mount Katahdin in Maine.

DWARF CINQUEFOIL (*Potentilla robbinsiana*)

Cinquefoils, which are pretty yellow members of the rose family, are fairly common sights in fields across the continent, but this particular species is one of the rarest flowers we have, since it grows only on Mount Washington in New Hampshire. Like other alpine wildflowers, it has hairy stems and small leaves and grows in small tufts; like most other cinquefoils, it has five yellow petals that surround numerous pistils and stamens. (The name cinquefoil means five-leaved.) An interesting contrast to the dwarf cinque-

foil is the rough cinquefoil, which grows erect, up to three feet in height. Since the rough cinquefoil inhabits fields in profusion it is considered a weedy nuisance.

DIAPENSIA (*Diapensia lapponica*)

Another low-growing wildflower plant that seems to create mats that stick closely to the rocky ledges where it lives is this very pretty native of the northeast. (It is also found in Lapland, hence its species name.) Like the dwarf cinquefoil, it is common above the treeline on Mount Washington, but it is also seen elsewhere, particularly in southern Canada. Its five-petaled flower superficially resembles the cinquefoil but it is not a member of the rose family, belonging instead to the very small diapensia group.

SUBALPINE BUTTERCUP
(*Ranunculus eschscholtzii*)

Buttercups are familiar blossoms in fields, on lawns, and in nearly every wild habitat imaginable, and they all resemble each other with bright yellow cuplike flowers, being quite difficult to distinguish even for the expert. This mountain member of the family has the largest flowers of all of the North American buttercups, so large in fact that they nearly obscure the leaves of this typical low-growing alpine plant, which is found in the Rocky Mountains from Alaska to New Mexico. Most buttercups grow in moist habitats, but this plant—and the sagebrush buttercup—have adapted to a drier existence.

MOUNTAIN PRIDE *(Penstemon newberryi)*

The penstemon group of flowers, members of the snapdragon family, are among the most beautiful wildflowers we have. Although there are a few species in the east, most of them are western plants, and many of them are found in the mountains. Typically, these alpine flowers grow in dense, matted clumps with long, narrow leaves. Penstemons come in many colors—blue-violet, white, red, and purple; this species has lovely deep pink flowers which bloom in midsummer, creating brilliant patches of color. The name penstemon comes from the fifth stamen, which is usually different from the others, having no anther but sporting a thick golden beard.

MOSS PINK *(Silene acaulis)*

Also known as moss campion, this beautiful member of the pink family is found in the tundra throughout the northern hemisphere and also on mountains as far south as northern New Mexico in the west and as far north as New Hampshire in the east. It somewhat resembles the purple saxifrage, for it too has pink flowers that grow from a thick mat of foliage, typical of most alpine plants. Sometimes these mats can be quite extensive, making a spectacular display when the flower is in bloom during midsummer. It is believed that the large number of red blossoms helps the plant to absorb and conserve heat, an important factor in this environment. For the same reason, the flowers often bloom on the south-facing side of the mat cushion in order to get as much sun as possible during the growing season.

Mountain Pride
(Penstemon newberryi)
Al Lowry

Moss Pink
(Silene acaulis; see page 78.*)*
Russ Kinne

ROADSIDE WILDFLOWERS

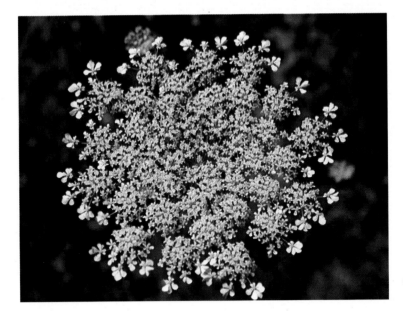

Queen Anne's Lace
(*Daucus carota*; see page 84.)
Townsend P. Dickinson

Although much of the American landscape has been altered over the past century with the creation of vast highway systems, farmland, cities, and towns, there is still some pleasure to be derived from a drive in the country, assuming one can stop along the way to observe the nature that has survived our efforts at progress. In fact, a close look at the typical American roadside can only make us appreciate the persistence of certain plants in the presence of gaseous fumes, dust, and litter. So far in this book we have met wildflowers hardy enough to withstand the incredibly difficult conditions posed by life in the desert, on the mountaintop, and deep inside the forest, but surely the hardiest plants of all are those that we find growing in profusion right under our noses, along our roads and in our vacant lots. Certainly we are grateful that they do manage to grow in such waste places, for they lend color, fragrance, and fascination to otherwise uninteresting or even ugly locations. It is a sad fact, however, that these wildflowers never seem to be appreciated very much. Farmers and gardeners call them weeds, and botanists tend to dismiss them as introduced species—plants that have escaped cultivation to displace native plants or to disturb the natural ecology of many regions. Like the Norway rat, the cockroach, and the starling, they are misfits that have become nuisances.

It is surely fitting that, in a book celebrating the beauty and power of the North American wildflower, we should set aside a short chapter to applaud a few of these hardy individuals. Not all roadside flowers were introduced from abroad; some are native plants that just seem to prefer living alongside human civilization rather than in the true "wild."

Ox-eye Daisies (*Chrysanthemum leucanthemum*; see page 84.)
S.J. Krasemann

Chicory
(*Cichorium intybus*; see page 86.)
Robert Bornemann

QUEEN ANNE'S LACE (*Daucus carota*)

This common flower is actually a Eurasian wild carrot, the ancestor of the carrots we eat today and a relative of parsley, celery, parsnips, coriander, caraway, and dill. (The taproot of this flower is edible, too, though it should be cooked first.) Because it reproduces so easily, it has become a troublesome weed in many parts of the world, and it has spread throughout most of North America, where it inhabits old fields and vacant lots as well as roadsides. The flat-topped "flower" is a head or umbel, consisting of several tiny white or pinkish flowers with a darker red flower in the center; after pollination, the umbels curl up, forming a fruit that resembles a bird's nest. The common name of this plant comes from the fact that in the eighteenth century, English courtiers would wear the flower as part of their costume.

OX-EYE DAISY (*Chrysanthemum leucanthemum*)

Many people are surprised to realize that this very common flower is actually not a native of North America but a European import, as is the shasta daisy, a close relative. (The cultivated chrysanthemum, derived from an East Asian species, is in the same genus.) Like yarrow, a native roadside plant and a member of the same family, the ox-eye daisy produces a distinctive flavor in milk if cows eat it and is thus regarded as a nuisance by farmers. Daisies are in the composite or sunflower family, which means that their flowers are really composites, consisting of sterile white ray flowers which attract insects to the fertile yellow disk flowers. The English daisy (*Bellis perennis*) is very similar in appearance; it, too, is imported but has become widespread in the west, reaching weed status like the ox-eye in some areas.

DANDELION (*Taraxacum officinale*)

Like the daisy, the ubiquitous dandelion is a composite flower with many yellow ray flowers; its toothed leaves must have reminded someone of a lion's teeth, which is how the common name, from the French *dent de lion*, came about.

Dandelion (*Taraxacum officinale*)
George E. Jones III

Canada Thistle (*Cirsium arvense*)
Angelina Lax

Although this flower, which blooms during the summer in the north and during winter in the south, is considered a common weed in pastures and lawns, it makes up for its nuisance value by being the source of salad greens; an excellent wine can also be made from the flower heads, which after pollination produce long silky bristles that can be blown off to carry their seeds in the wind. Birds like dandelion seeds, which they help to spread far and near. Because of the very deep taproot, dandelions are difficult to remove from the earth; again, however, there is some compensa-

tion, for the roots produce a milky sap that is said to have medicinal benefits. It is interesting that in Europe where the dandelion is native, this plant is not considered a weed but takes its "proper" place in the habitat.

CHICORY (*Cichorium intybus*)

Another member of the composite family, this too is an import that has become a pesty weed in some areas and that grows throughout the country in waste places of every description. The blue asterlike flowers last only a day, but just a few bloom at once, so the plant may lend an attractive appearance to the roadside for some time during the summer. Like the dandelion, the chicory has ways of compensating humans for its weediness (in fact, these may be the reasons the plant was originally introduced); its roots when ground and roasted can be used as a substitute for coffee or as a tasteful additive to it, and the plant is grown for this purpose both here and abroad.

CANADA THISTLE *(Cirsium arvense)*

This troublesome weed seems to be especially abundant in the fields and along the roadsides of the North American continent. The Canada thistle comes to us from Europe, via Canada, and is perhaps the most aggressive composite of all. The spines on its leaves and flowers make it unattractive to grazing animals, and new plants may grow from any section of its root, making it exceptionally difficult to eradicate. Its seeds are equipped with long bristly plumes, which makes it easy for the wind to carry them great distances. Nevertheless, the magenta flower heads, while small, are very pretty and fragrant, adding color to the landscape they inhabit.

RED CLOVER *(Trifolium pratense)*

Another magenta roadside flower is this very common clover, imported from Europe because of its usefulness as a pasture plant. It quickly escaped cultivation, however, and now can be found in lawns and fields across the continent. Because it stores nitrogen in its roots, it is often used to improve farmland, but we know it best as a source of nectar for honeybees, which, of course, help to spread it widely as they pollinate the clover blossoms. The flower is actually a head made up of tiny tubular florets, each with a drop of nectar at the base. In spite of its foreign origin, and probably because of its value to humans, it has received the distinction of becoming a state flower—in Vermont.

Canada Thistle *(Cirsium arvense)*
Earl Roberge

Red Clover
(*Trifolium pratense*; see page 87.)
James Hancock

BLUE VERVAIN (*Verbena hastata*)

The verbena family includes trees and shrubs as well as wildflowers, and teak is one of its most valuable species. The vervain flowers of North America are pretty plants that bloom in spikes or clusters and can be found throughout, often in old fields and along roadsides as well as in wilder areas of the continent. The spiky blue vervain illustrated here is attractive to bumblebees, and though it was once thought to have medicinal properties, it has no special value to humans. It is neither despised as a weed nor exploited for its usefulness; it is, in other words, a typical wildflower—pretty to look at and adaptable to an environment in which it plays an important if not especially noticeable role. The genus name, *Verbena*, means "sacred plant" in Latin (vervains were considered cure-all medications in ancient times), but we should take its name to heart and treat it—and all of its wildflower companions—as sacred, respecting their existence and protecting them from harm for their own sake.

As we have seen, wildflowers can perform marvels of survival in even the most hostile of habitats, but such adaptations usually take thousands of years; considering the rate at which humans are changing the face of the earth, destroying natural habitats as they go, we must make a special effort to be sure that the plants as well as the animals of the earth move into the future with us.

Blue Vervain (*Verbena hastata*)
John Bova

89

STATE FLOWERS

Alabama	Camellia	Montana	Bitterroot
Alaska	Forget-me-not	Nebraska	Goldenrod
Arizona	Giant Cactus Blossom	Nevada	Sagebrush
Arkansas	Apple Blossom	New Hampshire	Purple Lilac
California	Golden Poppy	New Jersey	Purple Violet
Colorado	Rocky Mountain Columbine	New Mexico	Yucca
Connecticut	Mountain Laurel	New York	Rose
Delaware	Peach Blossom	North Carolina	Dogwood
District of Columbia	American Beauty Rose	North Dakota	Wild Prairie Rose
Florida	Orange Blossom	Ohio	Scarlet Carnation
Georgia	Cherokee Rose	Oklahoma	Mistletoe
Hawaii	Hibiscus	Oregon	Oregon Grape
Idaho	Lewis' Mock Orange (Syringa)	Pennsylvania	Mountain Laurel
Illinois	Native Violet	Rhode Island	Violet
Indiana	Peony	South Carolina	Carolina Jessamine
Iowa	Wild Prairie Rose	South Dakota	Pasqueflower
Kansas	Sunflower	Tennessee	Iris
Kentucky	Goldenrod	Texas	Bluebonnet
Louisiana	Magnolia Grandiflora	Utah	Sego Lily
Maine	White Pine Cone and Tassel	Vermont	Red Clover
Maryland	Black-eyed Susan	Virginia	American Dogwood
Massachusettts	Mayflower	Washington	Rhododendron
Michigan	Apple Blossom	West Virginia	Rosebay Rhododendron
Minnesota	Pink and White Lady's Slipper	Wisconsin	Wood Violet
Mississippi	Magnolia	Wyoming	Indian Paintbrush
Missouri	Hawthorn		

SUGGESTED READING

There are many books about wildflowers, including both field guides and pictorial celebrations. The most lavish book is undoubtedly *The Audubon Society Book of Wildflowers*, published by Harry N. Abrams, with a text by Les Line, editor of *Audubon* magazine, and Walter Henricks Hodge and with beautiful full-color photographs by many of the world's prominent natural-history photographers. Although Denise Diamond's *Living with Flowers*, a Quill paperback published by William Morrow, contains much information about cultivated flowers, wildflowers are also included in her discussions of gardening and the uses of flowers in food, craft, medicine, and perfumes.

Of the field guides available, *The Golden Guide to Flowers* by Herbert S. Zim and Alexander C. Martin, published by Golden Press, is not comprehensive but has useful illustrations for the amateur. The two-volume *Audubon Society Field Guide to North American Wildflowers*, one on the east and the other on the west, is exceptionally comprehensive, with full descriptions of a great many species, together with full-color photographs, arranged by prominent color for easy identification.

INDEX OF WILDFLOWERS